Emotional Tanda

R. Maldonado de Grijalva

BookLeaf
Publishing

India | USA | UK

Presentation by *BookLeaf Publishing*

Web: www.bookleafpub.com

E-mail: info@bookleafpub.com

ISBN: 9789363314160

First edition 2024

Dedicated to the siblings who took on the role of parents while still wanting to enjoy a childhood.

I'm proud of all of us for continuing to move forward in life.

much love & respect.

- Rosie (Rose)

ACKNOWLEDGEMENT

Primeramente (first off), I would like to thank mi mami for birthing me into this world, and for demonstrating no matter what, to always love, forgive, and be humble.

- Thank you to all the strong and empowering women in my life who helped me keep my composure and build this composition.

- To my husband, a.k.a my "Gomez," and Chef Jesus Grijalva, thank you for supporting my every move, motivating me to be bold, do better, and teaching me to savor the flavors of life.

- Gracias a nuestra familia.
Thank you to all my siblings, in-laws, and cousins for growing and healing with me.
I am proud of all of us.

- Saving the best for last, I would like to thank you, the reader, not only for taking the time to read a part of me but also for your existence.

I am grateful for everyone who has walked with
me along the path of life, and I am thankful for
those I will one day encounter.

Con Amor,
Rosita

PREFACE

RuPaul says, "If you can't love yourself, how in the hell are you gonna love somebody else."

If you wish to do so, I ask you to be kind to your mind and love yourself as a whole.
Love yourself before anyone else.
To be confident, one must genuinely believe in themselves and value their self-worth.

Mahatma Gandhi once said, "Be the change you want to see in the world."
Change starts with oneself; work on your glow and radiate the energy you wish to attract.
Your emotions are energy in motion.

Throughout *Emotional Tanda*, there may be entries that may be sensitive to the reader.
All of these entries are from the writer's perspective & based on her life experiences.

[It is okay to put this book down if at any point in this book, you feel an unwanted emotion surface.]

Call her Rose

My name is Rosie, few know of me, and fewer know my story.

I am like an Edgar Allen Poe; my words convey their own flow.

To understand me the 'real me' can be an opportunity.

I stand by love, unity and sense of community, but please do not approach me if you hold any hostility.

I learned to love and care for myself, I found peace within, enough peace to learn to set a boundary.

Set a boundary, and you protect your energy.

Protect your energy and you begin to feel a state of serenity.

Depression is the consciousness' suppression.

I headed into a light of unknowing.
Each step forward, I felt a warmth glowing.
I felt hope, I felt positive.
My subconscious tapped in and said it is time to change my narrative.

So I did . . . .

Mind, Body, & Spirit

Inside me is a spirit that waits to live free.
Mother would say the outside world can be a
dangerous game, with time I learned it's best to
keep to myself rather than to experience shame.

I am no better than anyone but yesterday's
version of myself.
Who I once was, sits on a shelf.

I starved my ego to feed my spirit.
I became a Higher version of myself, for my
own satisfaction.

Mentally, I am grounded, and my emotions have stopped driving me.
Everything is processed more logically.
Physically, I began a 'self-love' journey.
I hug myself and express how much I love my body.
Spiritually, I wish to fly high beyond our sky, perhaps reach a deity's third eye.

Balanced mind, body, & spirit creates a beautiful harmony in you.
Be you, be true.

Love yourself before anyone else

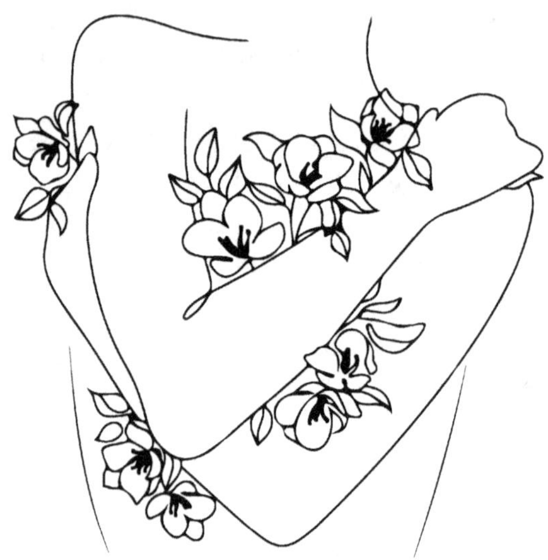

Their perception of my flaws, I acknowledge as
imperfections.
My imperfections are what makes me unique.
My uniqueness I see as perfection.

I do not compare myself to anyone other than
the broken being I was not long ago.
What must I prove?
Is it necessary to show all I know?
Regardless, I will grow, fast or slow.
Respectfully, love yourself & together let's glow.

Wish Good

She saw a bit of her reflection in everyone.
She saw good in those who were often
misunderstood.
If she saw that she could, she would.
See Good. Do Good. Be Good.

Set a boundary

'She's not the Rosie we fell in love with.'

For a moment I felt guilt, but why feel this guilt
if to them it did not matter how I felt.
They saw a side of me that was their perception
of pretty.
I set a boundary, and to them my actions were
perceived as ugly.
All I did was start caring for myself.

It was not their responsibility to stand by me or
help fix me.
It was fair to say it was not in me to seek a
friendship that had me feeling like I could no
longer breathe.

I cherish all the memories made, and all the gifts
exchanged.

As I grow, and as I heal, I confidently say I do
not hold any hatred for the things said.
I value my energy, and wish to protect my peace.
I set a boundary, and now my peace is sacred.

Smile now cry later

I would cry myself to sleep because I never
wanted anyone to see me weep.
Like my family, my thoughts run deep.
Thoughts so deep into my heart they seep.

Many believe crying makes you weak.
Yet, who are they to critique?
Does expressing this emotion really make you
weak?
In reality, expressing this emotion is just as
valid, and those who oppose are bleak.

May they think before they speak, and not see
crying as something weak.

Little Present

What is it that lets these emotions linger?
Is it really because all I could think of was their
little hand wrapped around my finger?
No. My thoughts were deeper. . . .
It was more than the universe not allowing me to
keep them.
As much as I was in denial, I accepted my fate,
and acknowledged deep down we were not
ready for their arrival.
This trial had me feeling suicidal.
I was at a point where I felt my soul had no
chance of revival.
We lost a little life, I cried.
I felt alone & all I wanted to do was hide.
I did not want anyone at my side.
I felt dead inside.
My hormones played games with my mind.

Took time to remind myself that life works in mysterious ways, and to not count but cherish the days.

Only moms understand

"If you had your own, you would understand the
pain mothers go through."

You are right, until I birth my own into this
world will I understand the physical pain
mothers go through.
You are right, my siblings are not my children
despite I caring for them like my own.
You are right, my mom could not be a good
mom.
She was too busy processing the death of her
father in another country, finding out her

husband was cheating on her, dealing with
postpartum depression and being pregnant with
her
4th child.
You are right, as a child I knew nothing.
All I knew was that someway I needed to help
my mom so we could survive and get by.

Your reality is different from mine.

My reality was that for a few years I was a
young mom to an unstable young adult mom.
I did not birth them, but I helped raise them.
I may not understand the physical pain of having
children, but I do understand the emotional pain
of raising them.

Not from here nor there

Our speech or grammar may not be perfect, but our hearts feel the same ambition & passions as our parents did the day they started their journey towards an
"American dream."
I am North American, born to native Hondurans.
Our parents are tired, so are we, in our own ways.

My mother taught me without saying anything.
I saw her struggle.
I saw her suffer.
Yet, I saw her never stop smiling.
In this country, it is a sin to not know English.

This is the land of the free for those who
practice Christianity, others may anticipate
scrutiny.
If our complexion is not fair, we are dirty.
At times I feel like an untouchable in this
unspoken caste system.

When I was five, I only knew how to speak a bit
of English.
I did not need anyone to translate to know I was
not welcome in my kindergarten class.
During lunch, one of my classmates spit at me,
and called me dirty.
Although I was born here, I felt I was not
worthy.

Over time I realized that self-worth is my
highest value.
It took time to learn how to love, accept, and
value myself.
I am North American, & I am living a different
American Dream.

A rule of society

A money hungry entrepreneur would say
"Unless there is something in it for me, don't
waste my time, my time is not free."
Time is money; if you don't come from old
money, or can't buy your place in society, you
are not worthy.
Upper class exposed me to this reality.

Either you look right enough to be a trophy wife,
or hustle and get yo money right.
Not making enough bread can make anyone go
crazy, enough to get knocked up and hope public
assistance funds them and they baby.
Plan B is to find a sugar daddy, but is it worth
trading in my sense of integrity?

Can't do that either because that's not how
momma raised me.

I'll just work and pray I will one day have a nine-figure salary, not so I can buy a spot in society, but to give back to my family.

Or More?

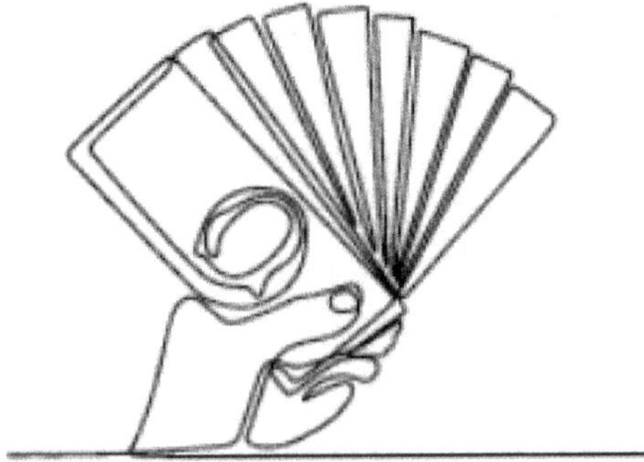

How much do you love yourself?

Do you love yourself as much as you love money?

Or more?

Do you value yourself like the value of currency?

Or more?

Is your worth as big as the bags you chase?

Or more?

Do you weigh your worth like the weight of gold?

Or more?

Do you cherish yourself like all the money in your world?

Or more?

Who is she?

She was an amateur model.
She was a novice photographer.
She was a makeup artist that wanted to be an
influencer.

She started to date, and put on weight.
She let herself go, lost followers she thought
were her friends.
She realized they did not care about her.

His [once] best friend called her a fat ugly pig
and told her she would never be an influencer.
Hearing him hurt, but he was right.

She deleted social media.
She lost interest in the number of followers.
She disconnected, and reconnected with the real
world.

Now she is learning to love herself the way she
has loved everyone else.
She became a realist.
She became a romanticist.
She became an artist.
She became someone she knows deserves to
exist.

My book of life

She is a woman her younger self wished should have had as a role model.

Someone to tell her it's okay to look different.
Someone to remind her to love herself even if she feels like the world around her does not want her.
Someone to hold her and reassure her she is not a burden, her life does matter, and to beg her younger self to stop hurting herself.
Someone to remind her to eat, & ask her to stop starving herself so she can be skinny.
Someone to remind her to be proud of her roots despite racists spitting in her face.
Someone to let her fall in love with who she wants to & not someone to "better her race."

Someone to tell her to follow her passions even when others told her she would not be anyone in life.
Someone to hand her violin after she put it down because her middle school teacher told her she would never be a real violinist.
Someone to hand her her camera and tell her to not give up on photography because she sees what others do not.
Someone to hand her her makeup brushes and remind her that makeup is an art and every artist has their own art style.
Someone to tell her " You got this mami. "

Life is not meant to be perfect, but it is meant to be lived.
I have made mistakes that became my life's greatest lessons.
Every day is a new day to continue to learn and grow.
Our reality is different for each other, and not everyone will have the same life experiences.
However, we can do better about being compassionate and possibly learn from each other.

As we continue to live life, perhaps look at life like a good book.

To get the full story, read from start to finish,
know that each chapter is a part of the story, and
to finish your book of life.

You cannot finish a book if you are stuck on a
chapter.

The flow of Rose

I embrace the spirit of a poet, and by now you
know of it.
At times, I have thought to quit, but I feel I have
a gift.
Few may understand how to flow, and maybe
fewer may learn to grow with their flow and
perhaps put on a show.
May my charisma glow and inspire others to
find their own flow.

Goddess Flora

Roman Goddess of spring and fertility, what joyous beauties you bring.
Symbol of love, beauty and abundance; such grace, such confidence.
Often associated with the beauty of a Rose, Flora, I thank you for your existence.

Tulips

Tulips. A beautiful flower that welcomes spring.
How fitting as tulips symbolize rebirth.
I pray for Earth's rebirth.
I pray for those seeking new beginnings.

We are not perfect, we are human, we all make
"mistakes."
A mistake occurs when you realize what you did
wrong and correct said mistake.
If this mistake is recurring, then it is no longer a
mistake, that is called a habit.

A tulip opens up when in direct sunlight.
Shine light on your life and open up a beautiful
version of yourself.

Rosaura

Before I was born, my mom loved the name
Aurora.
Instead she named me after my grandmother,
and nicknamed me Rosaura.

Oh Rosaura.
My Rosaura.
Sweet Rosaura.
Beautiful Rosaura.

I embraced this name and my aura.

Curse of Rose

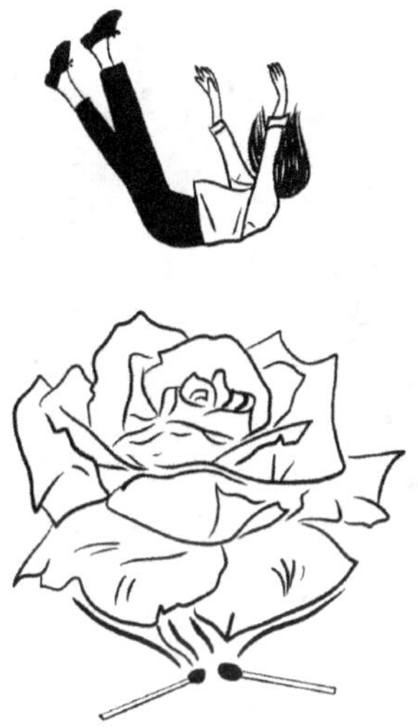

Part of life is accepting grief.
The moment we allow ourselves to grieve, is a moment our spirit may feel relieved.

What hurt most was being close and then our bond froze.
I call it the curse of Rose.

Round and Round her heart everyone goes, where they stop, she never knows.

Don't Go

Many times I sat on a bridge.
Many times I stood at a ledge.
Life had driven me to the edge.
Many times I felt it was time to leave this world.

What stopped me?
A possible domino effect on my family.

I am the oldest, in a way, I am a leader.
A part of me felt my family would follow my
lead.

How could I think so selfishly?
There would be pain from losing me, more so if
those that loved me realized I left willingly.

My [now] husband caught on.
He got in my face and demanded I tell him why
I thought he would want me gone.
He iterated how we had been together for this
long, and to continue to think like this was
wrong.
He held me and begged me, "Please be strong."

Because you're a girl

Actions will always speak louder than words.
Being a first born daughter seemed more like a
burden than a blessing.

My younger brothers did not realize they had
some privilege.
They could play outside, ride bikes, and climb
trees.
If mom ever saw me participating in any of these
activities she would discipline me on my knees.

My brother had a Game Boy that I was not
allowed to play because mom told him only
boys could play video games.
If mom saw me cry, she would tell me girls do
not play video games, and to go help clean.

I asked her why he could and not me.
'Because you are a girl, and for us it's a different
world.'
As a Girl, one must learn to cook, clean, and one
day care for her husband, end of discussion.

Naive at eighteen

I was young & naive.
If I got a tat for every mistake, I would be
covered head to toe.
I am not mad at what I did not know.
I was mad at those that assumed I was always
plotting.
How could I be plotting if I knew nothing.

I was young & naive.
All I really knew was to be someone's
housewife.

Momma & Auntie would tell me, "Get an education and don't depend on a man", but they would also tell me "You better know how to make tortillas and care for your husband."

Young and Naive at 18.
I learned quickly that the world is mean.
For some time, the life I live now felt like an impossible dream.
Life is not what it seems, it's up to you if you make your dreams your reality..

Mary is watching

Her mom raised her Catholic.
Anything that was not taught in catechism, mom
would deem Satanism.
She grew up close minded, raising her like this
sometimes had her misguided.
Mom did not want her to learn about the birds
and the bees.
Her only advice was to squeeze her knees
together, and that Mother Mary was always
watching her.
Putting an imaginary fear in her.

Let us pray

Let us pray for all things gay & pray God lights
their way so that the gay goes away.
When I first heard this, my mind thought
Matthew 19:14.

Are we not all children of God?
Are we not all to love thy neighbor?
Who is anyone to judge or think of themselves
as someone above others?

When they prayed, I also listened.
Let us pray we find peace someday.

Mother Mary

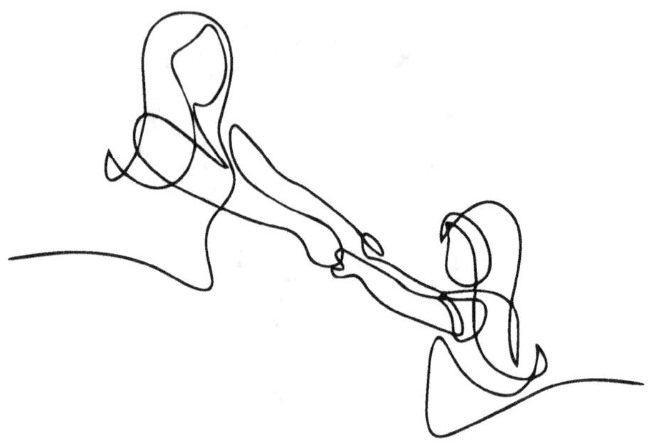

Blessed art thou among women. - A prayer to
Mother Mary-

Mother Mary, will I too be blessed if I part from
your ways?

Mother Mary, will I still be blessed if I love
someone who loves everyone & everything
except the corruption within religion?

Mother Mary, will I still be blessed if I share
your love outside of the church & not return?
Or will I be alone and someday burn?

Stay Humble

I am the daughter of immigrants, my mother is a housekeeper.

There is not much to me.

I am funny, I love being punny, and only God can judge me.

Since grade school, I helped my mom clean houses to help provide for the 5 of us.
I would dress myself with whatever got thrown out.
Mom was a freelance seamstress in Honduras, and she taught me I could repurpose clothes and make them my own.
I made my own style.

I went to a high school where students would
bully me or would say racist things to me.
I once dated this Russian, his adoptive mother
told him I needed to be with my own kind.

I would try hard to fit in, at times I felt I was not
the same person at school that I was at home.
While attending high school, mom would have
me clean houses by myself after school.
From what I earned, mom would let me save a
bit for dresses, and towards a violin.
I was usually finished cleaning no later than
7pm, just in time for church, prayer, bible study,
or choir practice.

We could not afford more than one car, so I
would often take buses and walk to where I
needed to go.
Rumors in our barrio (hood) started that I was
sleeping around.
Of course that was a lie..
I had homies I would play soccer or basketball
with, but that was all.

The homies would call me Fresa or Gringa, they
joked that I thought I was better than everyone.

Nah fam, I just had a lot on my plate, but also
mom forbids me to date if you are not at least
6'8.
Mom's house, mom's way, until the day I moved
away, now I live life my way.

Life, and family have taught me to stay out of
trouble, respect the hustle, and ALWAYS be
humble.

Family

Time and time again I hear you can pick and
choose your family.
Family is not only defined by blood.
I wonder, is it worth exchanging your peace or
maybe your sanity for bad blood?

We should not dwell in the past; we should
reflect, forgive, but not forget.
Reflect on the moments you struggled.
Even if for moral support, who stretched out
their hand to help instead of covering their
mouth as they spoke about you & your broken
family?

Who was there to feed you when you were
starving?
Who was there to clothe you when you outgrew
your clothes?
Who would make sure you had a warm shelter
on cold winter nights?
Who was there?

The one person that stayed behind was not even
a blood relative, but he cared for my siblings and
I as if we were his grandbabies.
I am grateful for him, and thanks to him, I
learned at a young age what a family should be.
Thank you for caring and watching over us
"grandpa."

Morning Times

Start my day with a cup o' joe at my favorite shop.
Anytime I am downtown, this is the place to stop.
Morning times is where I wrote most of these rhymes.
Morning times is where I can go to hear and see myself think.
Enjoy a delicious drink while you think.

I recommend a hibiscus ginger loose leaf tea with honey.

This entry was just to be funny.
(Not sponsored)

To be continued

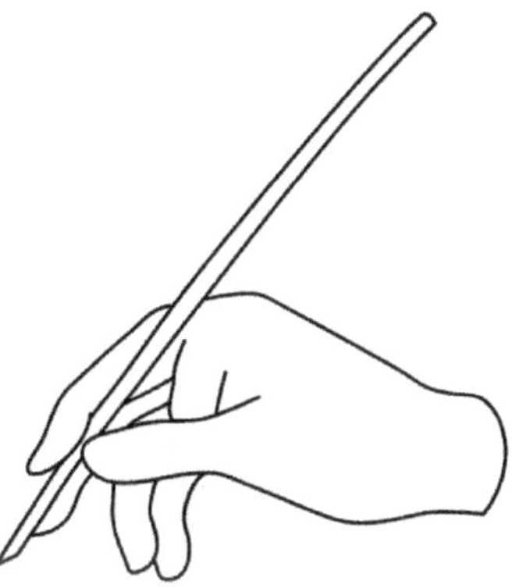

Who knew this is what 2024 got me into, nonetheless, I am glad I shared a bit of me with you.

I thank you for your time in reading this series of rhymes.
Let me know if you would like a 'part two'.

Peace be with you, and may you discover the truth in you.